This workbook is for you to learn, explore and embrace your tics

D1736613

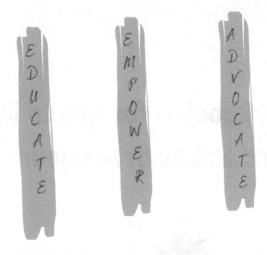

A massive thank you to

Ellen for helping me create this workbook,
Freya for her input into the flow and order,
Alison for giving me the confidence,
My boys, Harrison and Hayden for choosing me to be their mur
and allowing me to walk their Tourette's journey with them.
To my husband and youngest who keep me going each day,
striving to be the best I can be, for my family and tic community
Finally to all of you who took part in proof reading and adding
suggestions to make it perfect.

Let's Get started.......

Contents

Needed

Optional

About me

Let's start off by thinking about what makes you smile

All About Me

Self Portrait

Name

Birthday

Favourite colour

Favourite animal

Favourite food

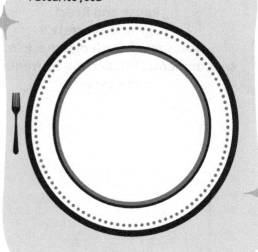

Hobbies

Favourite subject

Favourite place

What are tics?

To start, let's learn about tics!

By learning about tics, you will be able to understand how they work and also have the confidence to educate others if they were to ask you about them.
Throughout this workbook sometimes, I may use the words tic, and other times I may use the word Tourette's, but don't worry about that as I'm still talking about tics.

So what is a tic?

The definition of a tic is a sudden, rapid, recurrent, nonrhythmic, involuntary motor movement or vocalisation.
Tics can be motor (movements) and/ or vocal (sounds), but did you know they can also be mental (thoughts within your mind)

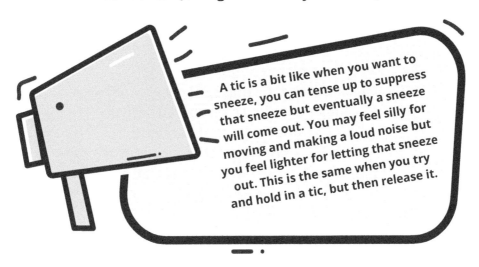

A tic is a bit like when you want to sneeze, you can tense up to suppress that sneeze but eventually a sneeze will come out. You may feel silly for moving and making a loud noise but you feel lighter for letting that sneeze out. This is the same when you try and hold in a tic, but then release it.

Tourette Syndrome is a common neurodevelopmental condition characterised by multiple motor tics and at least one vocal tic that have been present for longer than 12 months and started as a child.
Tourette syndrome is a genetic condition that causes individuals to make these involuntary sounds and movements called tics.

Genetic? I hear you say, but no one else tics in our family, you ponder.
Well, did you know that although it's genetic, it doesn't have to come directly from a relative who tics. It can come from other conditions such as ADHD, Anxiety or OCD for example.

Examples of tics

Tics usually start in childhood around age 7, however this can vary person to person. This can range from noticeable tics as a toddler to adult onset.

Common Motor Tics
Belly rolling/ Tensing
Blinking
Eye rolling
Facial Grimacing
Jerking of the head or other limbs
Shoulder shrugging
Tensing arms or legs
Touching objects or people

Common Vocal Tics
Coughing
Grunting
Sounds
Sniffing
Throat clearing
Tongue clicking
Repeating a sound, word or phrase.
Whistling

Not as Common Tics
Banging, smashing, hitting self/ others/ objects
Blocking (including speech and limbs)
Calling out (in / out of context)
Contextual tics
Inappropriate tics (swearing, racial, etc)
Snapping things
Spitting
Throwing things
Ripping up paper

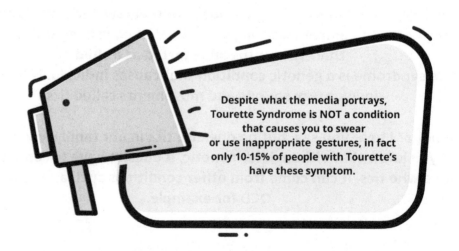

Despite what the media portrays, Tourette Syndrome is NOT a condition that causes you to swear or use inappropriate gestures, in fact only 10-15% of people with Tourette's have these symptom.

Mental Tics

Mental tics are sometimes called cognitive tics, and can often be confused as being intrusive thoughts.

Mental tics are exactly that - tics within your mind

Mental tics are often thoughts that play on loop, a bit like when we get the chorus of our favourite song stuck in our heads.

Mental tics can be totally random, they can be thoughts or images and they are usually very distracting.

Mental tics can be hard to explain to others but it's important you do let your family and friends know, if you experience them.

Pain and Tics

Tics can be painful, this could be because of the tic itself causing you to do something that hurts in the moment, or it could be due to the repetition, where the tic itself isn't causing pain, but because of doing it again and again and again, it can start to hurt.

Being in pain all the time from tics can have a negative impact on your mood, and day to day motivation to do things such as school work, hobbies and socialise. It's important that if your tics do cause you pain, that you let your parents, teachers and friends know, so they can help you and be understanding.

Seeing a chiropractor or having a sports massage can help with sore muscles and aching joints

4

Notes and Knowledge Check in

Can you remember what the definition of a tic is?

_____

_____

_____

Notes _____

_____

_____

_____

_____

_____

_____

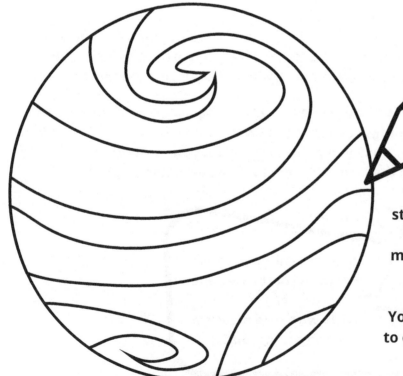

Tics can get worse when you're stressed or anxious. Taking part in activities that are relaxing like mindful colouring, can help reduce tics.

You will find several images for you to colour-in throughout this booklet.

Different Tic Conditions

There are different types of tic conditions, and these are identified by how your tics present for you.
Everyone who has tics will be affected differently.

Let's Explore.

TIC DISORDER OR TOURETTE SYNDROME?

PROVISIONAL (FORMALLY TRANSIENT) TIC DISORDER	PERSISTENT (FORMALLY CHRONIC) TIC DISORDER	TOURETTE SYDROME
SINGLE OR MULTIPLE MOTOR AND/OR VOCAL TICS	SINGLE OR MULTIPLE MOTOR OR (NOT BOTH) VOCAL TICS	SINGLE OR MULTIPLE MOTOR <u>AND</u> VOCAL TICS
LAST FOR ONLY A FEW WEEKS OR MONTHS AT A TIME	BUT THEY MUST LAST LONGER THEN 1 YEAR	MUST LAST FOR LONGER THEN 1 YEAR
AFFECTING AROUND 18% OF UNDER 10'S		THERE MUST BE A COMBINATION OF SEVERAL MOTOR TICS AND AT LEAST ONE VOCAL TIC

*There are also some other tic conditions but we wont go into them in this workbook, if you would like to explore them, you can search Functional tics and PANDAS via our website. www.tictocktherapy.co.uk

What is a premonitory urge?

A premonitory urge (PU), also known as a tic alert, is exactly that, an alert! It's the unpleasant feeling that comes before a tic happens. Many people say that the urge is worse than the tic itself. People describe the urge in different ways, here are some examples

Itchy

Pressure/
pain

Tingling

How does a tic happen?

In short, there is a glitch in our brains that causes a "tic alert" (premonitory urge).

This alert is sent to our bodies to let us know something is going to/ needs to happen. After we get the tic alert, we "tic"!
Once the tic happens, we get a relief from the urge, this then causes our happy hormone (dopamine) to be released and this sends feedback to our brain resulting in it knowing to do it again. This is called the tic cycle!!

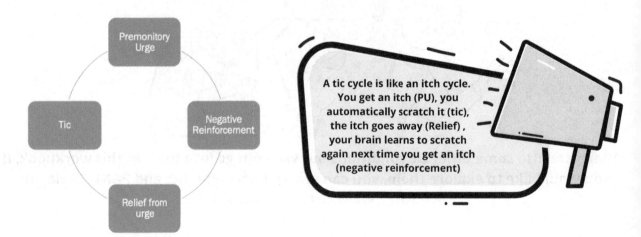

Premonitory Urge

Negative Reinforcement

Relief from urge

Tic

A tic cycle is like an itch cycle. You get an itch (PU), you automatically scratch it (tic), the itch goes away (Relief) , your brain learns to scratch again next time you get an itch (negative reinforcement)

Notes and Knowledge Check in

EDUCATE EMPOWER ADVOCATE

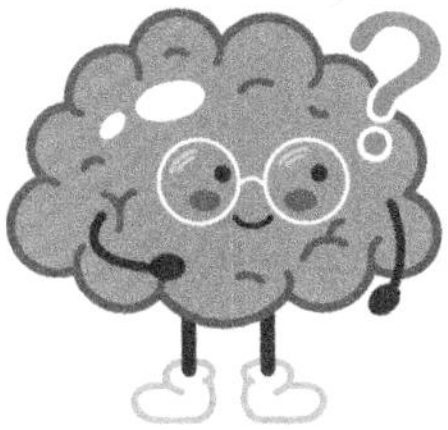

What types of tics do you need to be diagnosed with Tourette's?

Notes

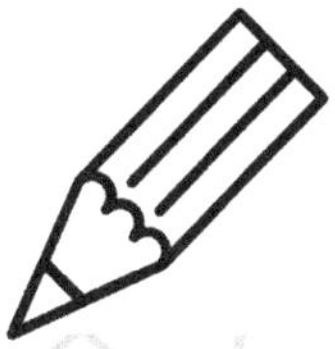

Are tics always visible?

Are tics always visible?.......
......Absolutely not!

And this is so very important to know, especially for people around you, such as parents and/or teachers. The reason it's so important is that an outsider may think you aren't experiencing tics much, if at all, therefore won't know that you could be struggling to focus or keep calm.

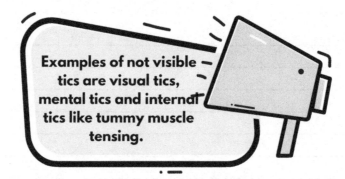

Examples of not visible tics are visual tics, mental tics and internal tics like tummy muscle tensing.

Fancy Names For Tics

Echolalia: Involuntary repetition of other's words and/ or phrases

Echopraxia: Involuntary repetition of other's actions

Echoskepsi: Involuntary mental repetition of something you have heard

Palilalia: Involuntary repetition of own words and/ or phrases

Palipraxia: Involuntary repetition of own actions

Paliskepsi: Involuntary mental repitition of own thoughts

Coprolalia: Involuntary repetition of obscene words and/or phrases

Copropraxia: Involuntary repetition of obscene gestures

Coprographia: Involuntary repetition of inappropriate words/ drawings

Coproskepsi: Involuntary mental repetition of inappropriate words/phrases

Where do tics come from?

I'm going to try and keep this really simple:

Tics are a neurological condition which means there is something that happens within our brains that causes tics to occur.

The part of the brain responsible for this is called the basal ganglia.
The basal ganglia is in charge of many different things, including our ability to 'stop'.
For example, to stop doing or saying something.

Those with tics are believed to have a slightly smaller basal ganglia then those who don't have tics.

It is also believed that those with tics, have too much of / or are super sensitive to a chemical called dopamine.

The easiest way to understand this is that our brain, is our brakes, and the dopamine is oil.

Between your slightly smaller brakes and excess oil, it's more tricky for us to stop these unwanted movements and sounds from occurring in the moment.

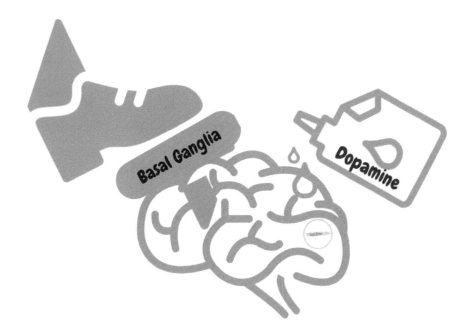

Note: there are other parts of the brain, and chemicals that can/may also play a part

Wordsearch time

```
S  E  A  S  T  B  R  R  C  T  I  C
N  E  U  R  O  L  O  G  I  C  A  L
I  N  V  O  L  U  N  T  A  R  Y  G
F  P  O  C  O  I  O  C  S  C  A  R
M  O  T  O  R  L  R  E  O  H  B  D
O  H  S  H  O  G  T  T  T  R  B  O
V  E  S  E  E  T  V  A  P  O  I  P
E  R  D  T  E  T  I  R  I  N  G  A
M  V  N  R  S  G  E  T  C  I  R  M
E  P  U  E  O  S  N  S  E  C  R  I
N  O  O  V  O  C  A  L  G  R  R  N
T  H  S  S  T  H  T  E  U  R  G  E
```

MOTOR	VOCAL	NEUROLOGICAL	TIRING
DOPAMINE	MOVEMENT	SOUNDS	INVOLUNTARY
TIC	URGE	TOURETTE	CHRONIC

Why do tics change?

As most of you will already know, tics can change all the time, they may change weekly, monthly, more or less. When these changes occur, it is called waxing and waning

Waxing = Tics increasing

Waning = Tics decreasing

Did you know that on top of the natural ups and downs of tic frequency, that our day to day life experiences can also impact where and when tic changes may occur.

Where we are
(EG: Home vs School)

Who we are with
(EG: are we comfortable to tic around them)

What we are doing
(EG: Do we like the activity)

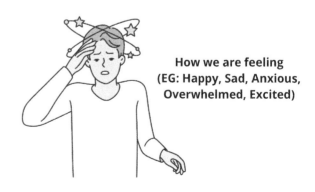

How we are feeling
(EG: Happy, Sad, Anxious,
Overwhelmed, Excited)

we will explore this more later in the workbook

What tics do you have/ have you experienced ?

Starting from the top of your head, down to the tip of your toes, note down what tic types you have now/ have had in the past.
Use one colour for past tics and a different colour for tics you have now.

Example: Toe scrunching

Challenge time

Draw a picture explaining how tics make you feel.
Do you have an urge before them? does it itch? does it ache?
Do you feel lonely, embarrassed, or scared?
Or do you embrace your tics? do they make you creative?

Crossword

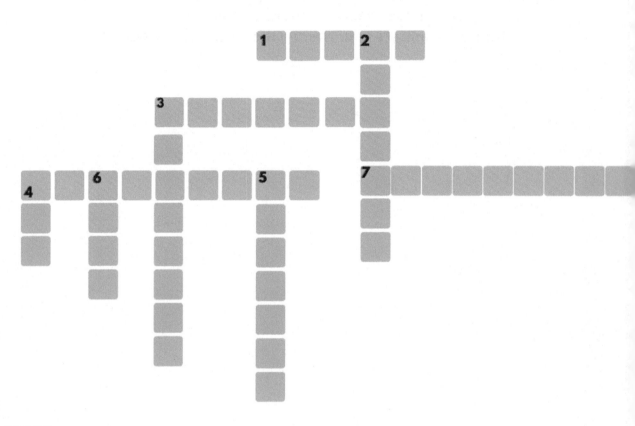

ACROSS
4) Motor and vocal tics for over a year
1) Tics use up a lot of energy
3) Motor or vocal tics for over a year
7) Motor and / or Vocal tics that last only a few weeks/ months

DOWN
6) The feeling before a tic
4) A sudden involuntary movement or sound
3) A positive trait of Tourette's
2) An emotion that can increase tic frequency
5) Common tic within the face

Common Co-Occurring Conditions

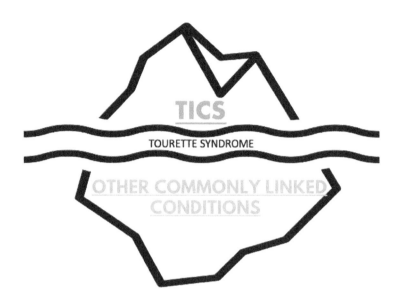

Tourette Syndrome is a condition in it's own entity, however in a very high proportion of those who have Tourette's, they will also experience symptoms from at least one other condition.

Attention-Deficit/Hyperactivity Disorder (ADHD), Obsessive-Compulsive Disorder (OCD) and Anxiety are the most common linked conditions with Tourette Syndrome (TS).

The next few pages will give a small insight to some of these conditons

Co-Occurring Conditions

Attention Deficit Hyperactivity Disorder (ADHD)

ADHD is the most common co-occurring condition for those with Tourette Syndrome (TS) with approximately 85% of those with TS also having ADHD and around 20 – 30% of children with ADHD also having a tic disorder.

ADHD is also diagnosed around the same age as TS, and also has a higher prevalence in boys like TS too.

ADHD may include, difficulty sitting still, constant fidgeting, moving, talking, making noises, have a low patience threshold, for example, they may find it hard to wait in a queue or listen, this can also result in them interrupting others.
They may also say and do things without thinking through the consequences due to their impulse control.

Types of ADHD & some examples of there characteristics:

Hyperactivity: noisy in play, fidgety, struggle to stay seated, always on the go, excessive talking, and say their brain never switches off.

Impulsivity: difficulty waiting turns, interrupts conversations, blurts out answers before question is completed.

Inattention: forgetful, poor organisation, distracted, loses things, appears to not listen, avoids tasks that require lots of attention, fails to complete tasks, makes careless mistakes

ADHD is often seen as a superpower, as ADHD brains work super fast and often think of great ideas on the spot.

Co-Occurring Conditions

Anxiety

Anxiety is common in most children at some point of their childhood. Anxiety is an emotion that gives us an unpleasant feeling within our body.
Anxiety is often temporary in children and can vary at different parts of their childhood.

Types of Anxiety & some examples of their characteristics

Generalised Anxiety Disorder: **Excessively worrying about a range of different things. i.e. future, family, friends or themselves. They may have difficulty in relaxing, they may also engage in challenging behaviour if expressing their feelings isn't possible.**
Separation Anxiety Disorder: **Children often go through this as a typical milestone, this anxiety appears when their parent leaves the room, but this usually stops around 30months old. If it's still present at school age it maybe worth seeking support.**
Phobias: **An irrational fear of something specific, these emotions are to the extreme and very intense. Individuals may avoid certain situations that enhance this fear. Children may engage in challenging behaviour if they cannot communicate their fear to people.**

Anxiety and Tourette Syndrome are closely interlinked, they form a cycle. Even if you're not an anxious person you may still experience the tic, anxiety cycle.

The tic, anxiety cycle starts when you

- **become anxious of other people seeing your tics**
- **This results in an increase of your tic frequency**
- **The increased tics results in an increase of anxiety and emotions**
- **The increased anxiety and emotions, increase your tics**
  and so on....
- **We mustn't forget that you're thinking about your tics throughout this cycle and this can also increase them because of the suggestibility.**

Routines and Predictability

Routines and having a predictable life can help manage anxious thoughts and unnecessary stress. How do you find mornings or evening with regards to your tics?

Create an ideal schedule for the day ahead each morning or even the night before to help yourself with anxiety and tic frequency.

TIME	TO DO	NOTES

Routines and Predictability

You may prefer to break your day into three parts, you can use this layout instead.

Co-Occurring Conditions

Obsessive Compulsive Disorder (OCD)

The symptoms of OCD are obsessions and compulsions.
Obsessions are uncontrollable thoughts, images, impulses, worries, fears or doubts.

They are often intrusive, (cause disruption and annoyance) unwanted and can be frightening for the person experiencing them.

Those with OCD will often know that these thoughts are irrational, but this doesn't mean they can control them. The most common obsessional thoughts are worrying about the safety of others or worrying that everything needs to be arranged symmetrically so that it is 'just right'.

Compulsions are purposeful behaviours and actions that are performed in an attempt to relieve the anxiety caused by obsessional thoughts. Often the behaviour is carried out according to certain rules, or will be performed as a ritual.

Relief provided by compulsions are only temporary and often reinforce the original obsession. Common compulsions include checking, counting and touching.

It can be difficult to tell the difference between a compulsion and a compulsive tic.

A compulsion is typically a behaviour that is carried out in an attempt to relieve anxiety that is caused by an intrusive or obsessional thought.

A compulsive tic is more associated with a physical sensation and needs to be performed to relieve the urge sensation.

Both can be as equally distressing!

Co-Occurring Conditions

Disinhibition

Disinhibition is when it becomes extremely difficult to use learned inhibitory (brain breaking) skills in the moment.

Disinhibition is very common in those with Tourette's and / or ADHD
It is important to know that these behaviours are part of Tourette Syndrome and they are not deliberate.

Individuals with Tourette Syndrome can often appear to be overstepping the mark and impulsive. This is because of disinhibition!

Even though many individuals will know that what they are doing/ saying is inappropriate at the time, they are not able to put on the brakes to these behaviours in that moment.

Essentially, your brain likes to run ahead of you before you can put your foot on the breaks.

Understanding disinhibition is essential in understanding Tourette's!

The disinhibition element of Tourette's can be a big problem within school, I bet many of you can think of a time you have been "pulled" up on a behaviour that wasn't necessarily a tic but you couldn't help it?

It is also important to know, that just like tics, disinhibited behaviours can also be suggestible. So, reminders of desired behaviours are more likely to cause the undesired behaviours.

A great skill to learn to manage disinhibition, anxiety, being impulsive oand reacting to quickly is to

PRACTICE

PAUSING

Counting to 3 or 5

BEFORE

REACTING

Games like Simon say's are a great way to improve your brain breaks when it comes to acting on impulse

Co-Occurring Conditions

Rage and Tourette's

Feeling out of control of your emotions , and/ or your body can be very frustrating. It's not a huge shock that those with tics can become easily frustrated and overwhelmed.

It is very common for an individual to struggle to explain why they have had an anger outburst and sometimes the episodes of anger can occur very quickly (0 - 100). It may also seem like there was little cause for the outburst for someone watching.

It is believed that people with tics and those who are easily angered, may be because of some of the following reasons

1. **Rigid thinking**
2. **Struggle to manage change of plans**
3. **Low frustration level**
4. **Easily over-stimulated and over-whelmed (too loud, too bright etc)**
5. **Frustrated or feel embarrassed by the events**
6. **Anxiety**

Anger is more likely when you feel tired, when at home from school or other places and is most likely to be directed at mothers, fathers and brothers and sisters.

Did you know? ANGER comes from the same place as ANXIETY & DEPRESSION

Notes and Knowledge Check in

Are all tics due to Tourette's?

Notes --

Environmental Factors and tic frequency

As mentioned earlier on in this workbook, environmental factors can impact tic frequency and severity.

Common, often spoken about, environmental factors often consist of:
Where you are, home vs school, or if you have anxiety or stress at that moment.

But did you know the following can also have a huge impact on your tic presentation.

Sensory input

Tiredness

Mood

Food and Drink

Friendship issues

Emotions

People (who you're with)

Illness

Exams

Did you also know that how you have previously been responded to with your tics in that setting or by that person can all have an influence to, In fact anything can impact tic frequency.

Let's Explore

When are your tics better?	**When are your tics worse?**

Don't worry if you can't think of any yet, add them as you find out what they are by paying attention to your tic frequency and your environment from today onwards.

Think about different places: Home, School, Shops, Alone in bedroom...

Think of different people: Parents, Friends, Teachers, Strangers...

Think about Emotions: Happy, Sad, Excited, Anxious, Apprehensive...

Think about sensory input: too loud, too quiet, too bright, too dark, hungry, thirsty, being too hot or too cold.

Think about what happens if you eat certain things: too much sugar, too much caffeine, too spicy...

Think about different activities you do, different lessons...

Triggers & Reinforcers

Another way to find patterns in what triggers or reinforces your tics is by completing a form like this below. keep a log every time your tics change (increase or decrease) for 2 or more weeks and then go through and see if you can find any patterns. There are some examples on the next page.

Before	What ?	After
Add here: Day, time, what you were doing, who you were with, were you enjoying what you were doing? were you asked to do something you didn't want to do, were you hot/cold, hungry/ thirsty, anxious/ excited, did someone notice your tics or ask you to be quiet	Add here: What happened! Tics increased, decreased, changed from motor to vocal, tic attack, seizure, limb lock	Add here: What happened during/ after your tic change? Did someone come and see if you're ok? offer you a drink? panic? did they get annoyed at you? did you stop the task you were doing/ about to do? how did you feel about it after? (carry on as normal, get annoyed/ upset ...)

Triggers & Reinforcers

Common patterns when exploring tic triggers and reinforcers using a 'Before & After log' can be seen below. Remember triggers and reinforcers will be different for everyone. There is no right or wrong answer.

Tics worse on Sundays when you have school the next day. (likely due to school based anxiety) Try and work out what it is about school that causes this anxiety.

Tic Attacks happen more when with certain friend(s), family member. (likely due to that person(s) giving you more attention or you being more anxious regarding your tics when with them)

Tic increase/ Attack or seizures always seem to occur between two times, eg: 10am and 1230pm (likely due to hunger/ fatigue) try scheduling rest and snack breaks

Symptoms always worse once in bed (likely to be linked to your mind being unfocused or anxiety) try listening to story/ music/ podcast to help you focus your attention away from tics/ anxiety.

Non Epileptic Seizures / Tic Attacks only happen in one environment (eg: home vs school) did you know its very likely the people/ emotional link that environment causes this.

Remember by finding triggers & reinforcers you can learn to control/ change them to manage your tic frequency.

Tics always worse when waiting in anticipation to speak / do something or being put on the spot. This is linked to anxiety and fear of being embarrassed or getting it wrong. Try asking your teacher to not call on you to answer questions in class and see if this helps.

Let's Rate Your Triggers

Let's explore how much different places/activities may raise your anxiety, and tic frequency. Draw a line to where on the scale, each example affects you, and add any extra ones you can think of.

Brushing your teeth

Car trips

Dentists

Having visitors in the house

Eating lunch in school hall

Eating dinner with family

Getting hair cut

School

Being put on the spot

_____

_____

_____

_____

_____

_____

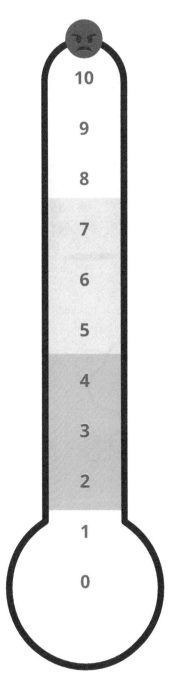

Now let's explore why this may be?

Have a think about all the times you have felt a tic shift in the environments stated on the previous page. What thoughts are running through your mind? Is there anything you can put your finger on as to what it is that causes this change?

"I hope they don't notice my tics", "What if they ask me questions about them"

"What if they tell me off again"

"I'm always so tired in this room"

_____

_____

_____

_____

_____

_____

_____

_____

_____

_____

Changing Environmental Triggers

When you know where and why different 'things' change your tic frequency, you can start exploring how you can change the environment to reduce the impact it has on your tics.

Trigger

EG: What if they ask me a question about my tics?

What can we change

EG: Educate my peers so they understand how tics work and are much less likely to ask me a question

Safe places

Learning where your tics are 'good' or 'bad' is a great way to stay in control of your environment and know where your 'safe places' are. It's always good to start brain dumping your thoughts around different places. To get you started, think about eating out and fill in the grid

-Restaurants -

😄 =Happy to go here anytime
🙂 = Depends on my tics, mood etc
☹ = Tics always bad here

Rating	Restaurant Name	Notes
😊	EG: McDonalds	Relaxed, lots of hustle & bustle so I blend in. can eat with fingers

Safe places

Ok now you have practiced with different places to eat out, go ahead and think about anywhere you go regularly or maybe somewhere new
- Other Places -

☺ =Happy to go here anytime
😐 = Depends on my tics, mood etc
☹ = Tics always bad here

Rating	Type of place	Notes

Notes and Knowledge Check in

What can be done to reduce tics?

Notes ------------------------------------

start here

Coping with other peoples questions and stares

How do you currently feel whilst ticcing around others?

Parents/ Siblings

_____

_____

_____

BE HONEST

School Friends

_____

_____

_____

Other family

_____

_____

_____

Strangers

_____

_____

_____

Acquaintances

_____

_____

_____

Teachers

_____

_____

_____

Often, it's not the actual tics that worry people.

They're more worried about how others may act/ what they may say.

Coping with other peoples questions and stares

<u>**REMEMBER: You can only control**</u>

<u>Your</u> thoughts, feelings,
non tic-movements, reactions,
non tic- vocalisations or anything in
between

<u>**REMEMBER: You cannot control**</u>

<u>Other</u> people's thoughts, feelings,
movements, reactions, vocalisations
or anything in between

Write down any questions you have ever been asked about your tics, or, any situations where people have looked at you because of them that triggered your own thoughts

----

Coping with other peoples questions and stares

Many people with tics state that it isn't the tics that bother them in public, it's the uncertainty of what someone may ask them and them not knowing how to reply.

Is this the same for you? (circle your answer)

Now you're hopefully feeling more educated on tics, I would like you to think about some ways you can reply to common questions you have been asked in the past. Write them (your replies) below.

"   "
_____

"   "
_____

"   "
_____

"   "
_____

"   "
_____

"Oh, thats a tic, I do it often, have you only just noticed"

" It's a tic, I have Tourette Syndrome"

"Tourette's is a neurological condition which causes me to move or speak with out my full control"

EXAMPLE'S

<u>Coping with other peoples questions and stares</u>

Now you have some pre planned reply's to common questions, memorise your favourite and get practising.

Ask your family and friends to ask you questions so you gain confidence in educating others and advocating for yourself.

Remember some days it will be easier than others, but as long as we are taking steps in the right direction, it doesn't matter how small they are.

PROGRESS Not PERFECTION

one small step forward, is better than no step at all

Challenge time

Create your own question sheet and test your friends and family on their knowledge of tics and Tourette's. Maybe create a fact sheet first and allow them to revise before hand.

Family and Friend Quiz

Questions:

1)_____

2)_____

3)_____

4)_____

5)_____

6)_____

7)_____

8)_____

9)_____

10)_____

Remember to keep a note of the answers for your reference

Notes and Knowledge Check in

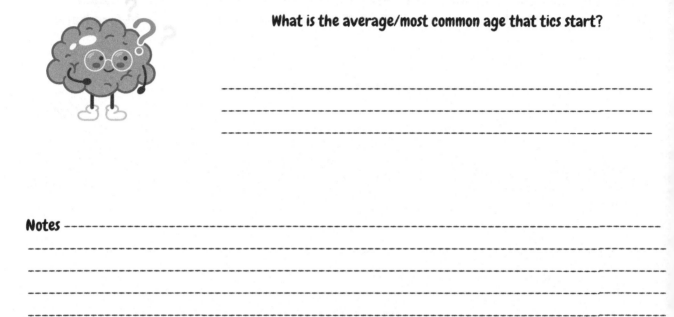

What is the average/most common age that tics start?

_____
_____
_____

Notes --

STAY ACTIVE!

Go and do something super active for 10 minutes and then write down what you did, how it made you feel and if it made a change to your tic frequency --
----

Emotions and Feelings

Our emotions and feelings can impact <u>everything</u> we do each day.

As we already know from the previous pages our emotions can also impact our tic frequency and severity.

Therefore, being able to understand and manage our emotions is really important.

It's also really important that we are honest about how we are feeling and that we don't just put on a brave face to please others.

The next few pages are some activity's to help you get your thoughts out of your mind and on paper.

This can help open up conversation with others about what's going on for you and your emotions but most importantly it will help empty your feelings bucket from within.

Emotions and Feelings

Normalising Emotions and feelings

Talk about mood/ emotions and feelings as though you're chatting about the weather. Make it part of your everyday conversation. Ask how others are, and tell them how you're feeling.

How are you doing?

What's up?

HOW ARE U?

How's everything?

How's it going?

REMEMBER!

It's OK NOT TO BE OKAY

Communicate with others! Don't Isolate yourself.

Good things Diary/Tracker

Every evening before bed, write down three things from your day that made you happy/smile. Some days it might be hard but I want you to make sure you find something, no matter how small each and every day.

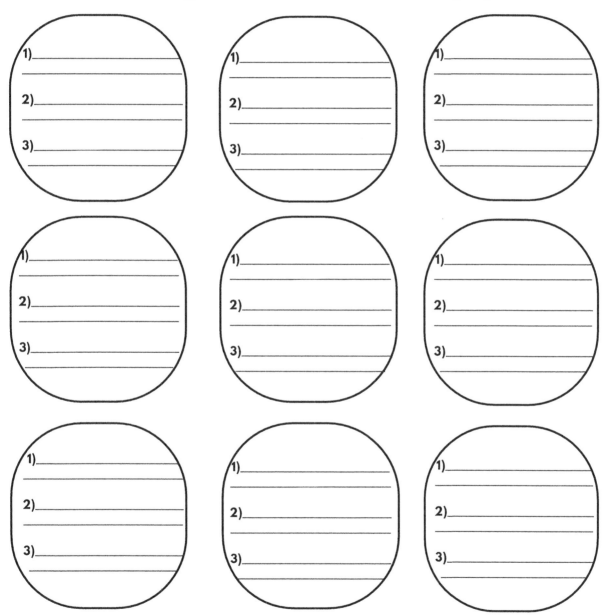

Focusing on the good parts of our day, creates more happy chemicals in our brain and helps with our mood, anxiety and levels of overwhelm. There are extra sheets at the back to keep a journal.

Emotions and Feelings

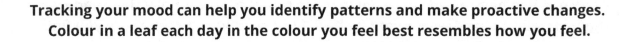

Tracking your mood can help you identify patterns and make proactive changes.
Colour in a leaf each day in the colour you feel best resembles how you feel.

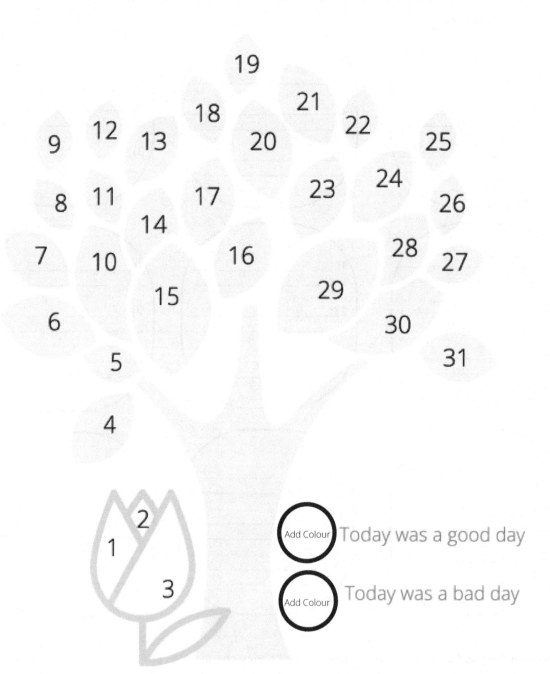

Add Colour — Today was a good day

Add Colour — Today was a bad day

Brain Dumping

Brain Dump each morning to help reduce the load inside your mind and body

What am I looking forward to today?

What is worrying me? Making me grumpy today?

to do

Today's Happiness Scale

1   10

Today's Tic Scale

1   10

Today's Tiredness Scale

1   10

Positive Affirmations

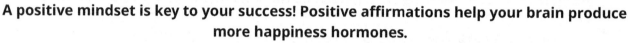

A positive mindset is key to your success! Positive affirmations help your brain produce more happiness hormones.
Create your own positive affirmations on the next page.

I matter

I deserve good things

I believe in me

I am amazing

I can make a difference

I am brave

I can do this

I am beautiful

I bring peace

I am kind

I am a fighter

I am loved

Positive Affirmations

A positive mindset is key to your success!
Fill the page with positive affirmations about yourself.
Read it to yourself each morning and evening.

RELAX
MODE ON

The next few pages show some different ways to help relax and ground yourself

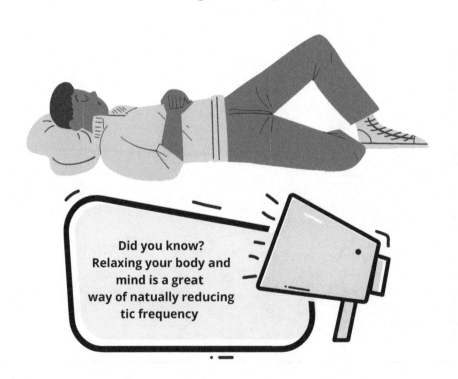

Did you know?
Relaxing your body and mind is a great way of natually reducing tic frequency

Reducing tics

Below is a list of activities that you might find useful for reducing stress and helping you to relax.
Try introducing some of these into your daily routine and see if they help reduce your tics.

Yoga
Meditation
Deep breathing
Mindful colouring
Spending time in nature
Massage
Weighted blankets
Reading
Taking part in sports
Listening to music
Playing an instrument or singing
Going for a walk

Reducing tics by keeping your brain busy and focused

Did you know that engaging your brain can help to reduce tics? Activities like learning to play an instrument, taking part in sports, listening to music, solving puzzles, meditation, going to the gym, drawing, painting and many other activities can calm an overactive brain, this works by giving your brain something else to focus on.

Are there any activities that reduce your tics? Make a list below of what helps, and then make a seperate list of activities you might like to try.

What helps?

_____

_____

_____

_____

_____

_____

What would you like to try?

_____

_____

_____

_____

_____

_____

Balloon breathing exercise.

For this activity you are going to imagine that your lungs are the ballon inside of you.
As you breath in, you are filling the balloon (your lungs) with air.

As you breath out you are gently pushing the air back out of the balloon.

Repeat this 5 times.

HOT CHOCCY BREATHING

This is a great way of focusing your breathing whilst doing your school work. Imagine you have the best ever smelling hot chocolate sat on the desk in front of you, between you and your school work.

It smells like the best hot chocolate you have ever smelt, so make sure you take long, slow breaths in through your nose to suck up all those amazing smells.

BUT

It's far too hot to drink yet, so we need to blow on it to cool it down.

Keep repeating this during your school work to help keep your mind calm and focused

5-4-3-2-1
Grounding Technique

This calming technique connects you with the moment by exploring your five senses.

Look around where ever you are, take a deep breath in and find.....

5 | 5 things you can see

4 | 4 things you can touch

3 | 3 things you can hear

2 | 2 things you can smell

1 | 1 thing you can taste

Hand Breathing

Hold your hand out in front of you.

Use your index finger from your other hand, then really slowly trace up and down your fingers.

As you trace up your finger, breath in through your nose, as you trace down, breath out through your mouth.

Repeat (whole hand) 3 - 5 times

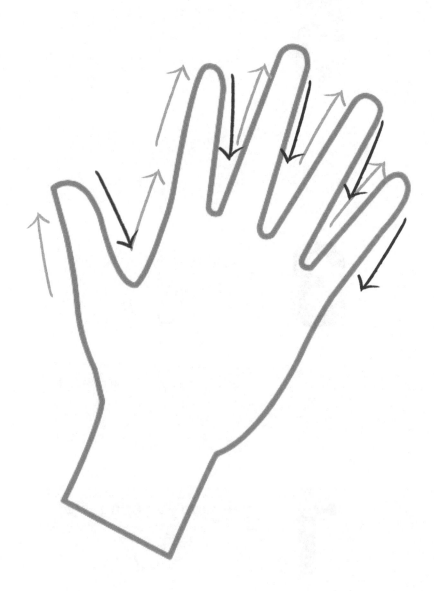

Power of Catch

When we are stressed, overwhelmed, anxious, worried and so on, it's very likely that the thinking part of our brain is taking a nap.

It's really hard to calm down or think clearly when this part of our brain is sleeping.

A great way to wake it up is to play catch. Your family can help here by starting it off but as you get better at noticing when your thinking part of your brain is napping, you will be able to play catch with yourself and get the same results.

What are my coping strategies?

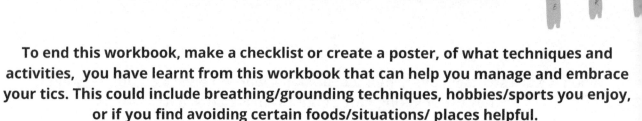

To end this workbook, make a checklist or create a poster, of what techniques and activities, you have learnt from this workbook that can help you manage and embrace your tics. This could include breathing/grounding techniques, hobbies/sports you enjoy, or if you find avoiding certain foods/situations/ places helpful.
Keep this page visible to remind yourself how to manage and remain confident moving forward.

Remember

Moving forward, your tics do not define you!
Educate those around you!
Learn your triggers and manage them to the best
of your ability by making changes!
Last but not least go and tic loud and proud if you
want to.

The next few pages have spare worksheets and question answers

Triggers & Reinforcers

Another way to find patterns in what triggers or reinforces your tics is by completing a form like this below. keep a log every time your tics change (increase or decrease) for 2 or more weeks and then go through and see if you can find any patterns. There are some examples on the next page.

Before	What?	After
Add here: Day, time, what you were doing, who you were with, were you enjoying what you were doing? were you asked to do something you didn't want to do, were you hot/cold, hungry/ thirsty, anxious/ excited, did someone notice your tics or ask you to be quiet	Add here: What happened! Tics increased, decreased, changed from motor to vocal, tic attack, seizure, limb lock	Add here: What happened during/ after your tic change? Did someone come and see if you're ok? offer you a drink? panic? did they get annoyed at you? did you stop the task you were doing/ about to do? how did you feel about it after? (carry on as normal, get annoyed/ upset ...)

Triggers & Reinforcers

Another way to find patterns in what triggers or reinforces your tics is by completing a form like this below. keep a log every time your tics change (increase or decrease) for 2 or more weeks and then go through and see if you can find any patterns. There are some examples on the next page.

Before	What?	After
Add here: Day, time, what you were doing, who you were with, were you enjoying what you were doing? were you asked to do something you didn't want to do, were you hot/cold, hungry/ thirsty, anxious/ excited, did someone notice your tics or ask you to be quiet	Add here: What happened! Tics increased, decreased, changed from motor to vocal, tic attack, seizure, limb lock	Add here: What happened during/ after your tic change? Did someone come and see if you're ok? offer you a drink? panic? did they get annoyed at you? did you stop the task you were doing/ about to do? how did you feel about it after? (carry on as normal, get annoyed/ upset ...)

Triggers & Reinforcers

Another way to find patterns in what triggers or reinforces your tics is by completing a form like this below. keep a log every time your tics change (increase or decrease) for 2 or more weeks and then go through and see if you can find any patterns. There are some examples on the next page.

Before	What ?	After
Add here: Day, time, what you were doing, who you were with, were you enjoying what you were doing? were you asked to do something you didn't want to do, were you hot/cold, hungry/ thirsty, anxious/ excited, did someone notice your tics or ask you to be quiet	Add here: What happened! Tics increased, decreased, changed from motor to vocal, tic attack, seizure, limb lock	Add here: What happened during/ after your tic change? Did someone come and see if you're ok? offer you a drink? panic? did they get annoyed at you? did you stop the task you were doing/ about to do? how did you feel about it after? (carry on as normal, get annoyed/ upset ...)

Safe places

Ok now you have practiced with different places to eat out, go ahead and think about anywhere you go regularly or maybe somewhere new
- Other Places -

☺ =Happy to go here anytime
😐 = Depends on my tics, mood etc
☹ = Tics always bad here

Rating	Type of place	Notes

Safe places

Ok now you have practiced with different places to eat out, go ahead and think about anywhere you go regularly or maybe somewhere new
- Other Places -

☺ =Happy to go here anytime
☺ = Depends on my tics, mood etc
☹ = Tics always bad here

Rating	Type of place	Notes

Safe places

Ok now you have practiced with different places to eat out, go ahead and think about anywhere you go regularly or maybe somewhere new
- Other Places -

☺ =Happy to go here anytime
☺ = Depends on my tics, mood etc
☹ = Tics always bad here

Rating	Type of place	Notes

Good things Diary/Tracker

Every evening before bed, write down three things from your day that made you happy/smile. Some days it might be hard but I want you to make sure you find something, no matter how small each and every day.

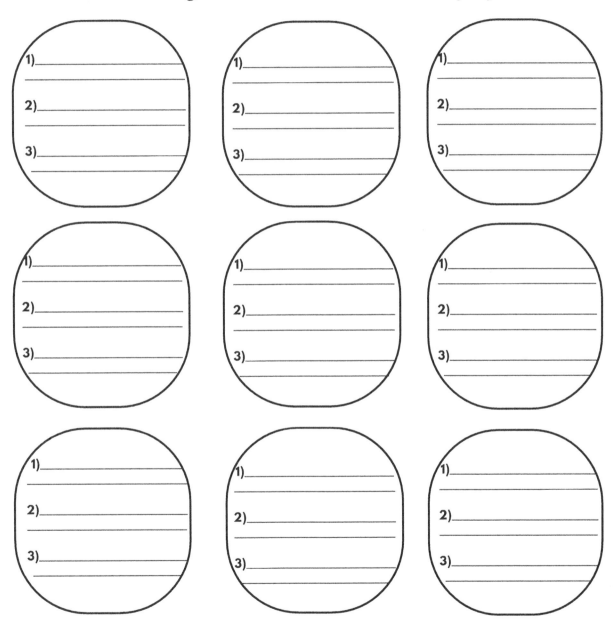

Focusing on the good parts of our day, creates more happy chemicals in our brain and helps with our mood, anxiety and levels of overwhelm.

Good things Diary/Tracker

Every evening before bed, write down three things from your day that made you happy/smile. Some days it might be hard but I want you to make sure you find something, no matter how small each and every day.

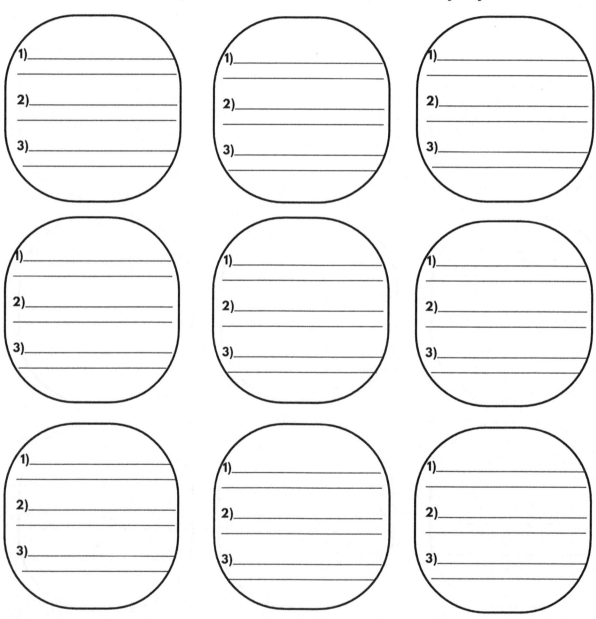

Focusing on the good parts of our day, creates more happy chemicals in our brain and helps with our mood, anxiety and levels of overwhelm.

Good things Diary/Tracker

Every evening before bed, write down three things from your day that made you happy/smile. Some days it might be hard but I want you to make sure you find something, no matter how small each and every day.

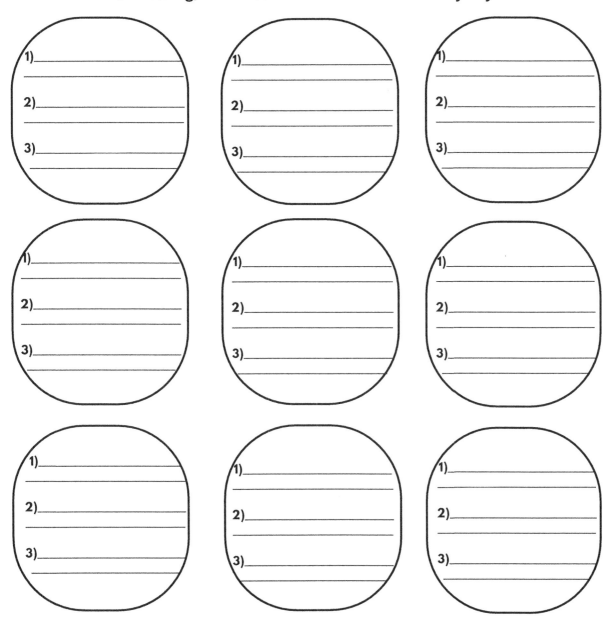

Focusing on the good parts of our day, creates more happy chemicals in our brain and helps with our mood, anxiety and levels of overwhelm.

Emotions and Feelings

Tracking your mood can help you identify patterns and make proactive changes. Colour in a leaf each day in the colour you feel best resembles how you feel.

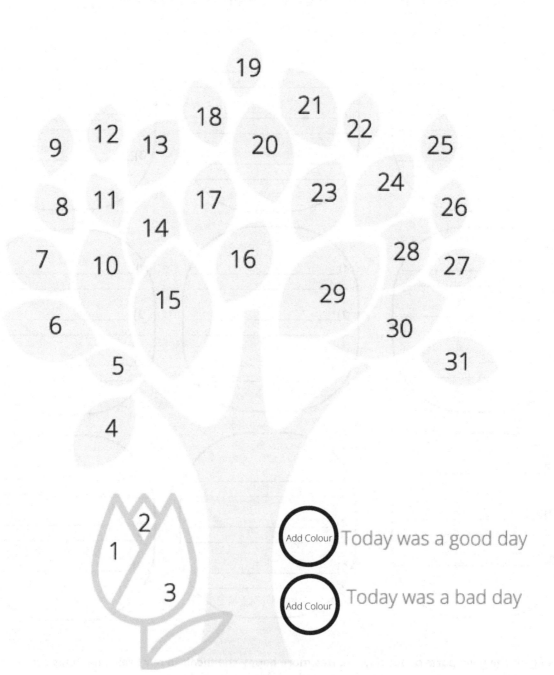

Add Colour — Today was a good day

Add Colour — Today was a bad day

Emotions and Feelings

Tracking your mood can help you identify patterns and make proactive changes.
Colour in a leaf each day in the colour you feel best resembles how you feel.

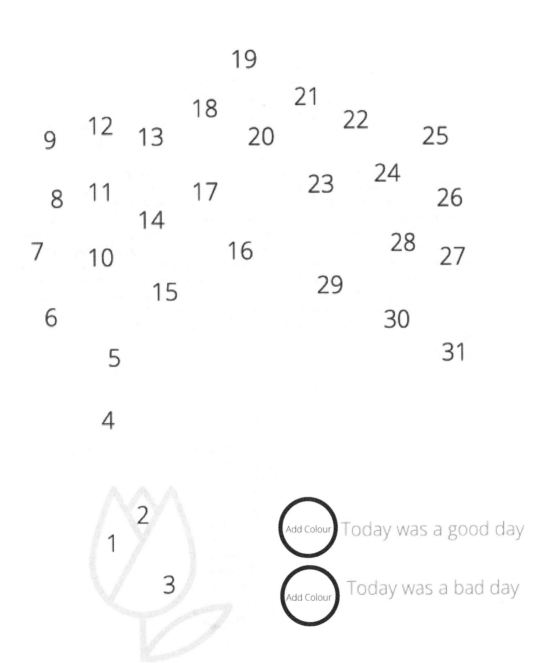

Add Colour Today was a good day

Add Colour Today was a bad day

Emotions and Feelings

Tracking your mood can help you identify patterns and make proactive changes.
Colour in a leaf each day in the colour you feel best resembles how you feel.

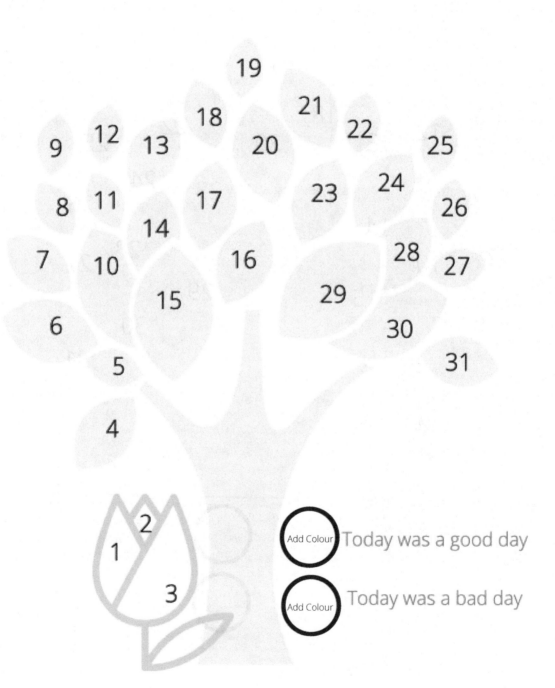

Add Colour — Today was a good day

Add Colour — Today was a bad day

Brain Dumping

Brain Dump each morning to help reduce the load inside your mind and body

What am I looking forward to today?

What is worrying me? Making me grumpy today?

to do

Today's Happiness Scale

1   10

Today's Tic Scale

1   10

Today's Tiredness Scale

1   10

Brain Dumping

Brain Dump each morning to help reduce the load inside your mind and body

What am I looking forward to today?

What is worrying me? Making me grumpy today?

to do

Today's Happiness Scale

1 ★★★★★★★★★★ 10

Today's Tic Scale

1 ★★★★★★★★★★ 10

Today's Tiredness Scale

1 ★★★★★★★★★★ 10

Brain Dumping

Brain Dump each morning to help reduce the load inside your mind and body

What am I looking forward to today?

What is worrying me? Making me grumpy today?

to do

Today's Happiness Scale

1   10

Today's Tic Scale

1   10

Today's Tiredness Scale

1   10

Routines and Predictability

Routines and having a predictable life can help manage anxious thoughts and unnecessary stress. How do you find Mornings or evening with regards to your tics?

Create an ideal schedule for the day ahead each morning

TIME	TO DO	NOTES

Routines and Predictability

Routines and having a predictable life can help manage anxious thoughts and unnecessary stress. How do you find Mornings or evening with regards to your tics?

Create an ideal schedule for the day ahead each morning

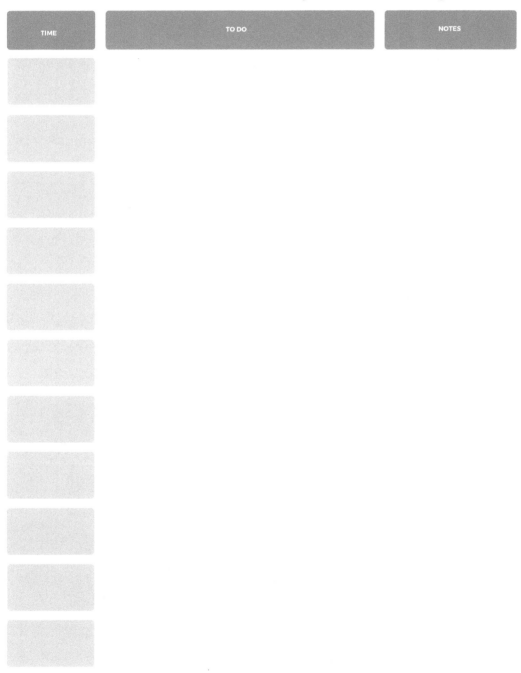

TIME	TO DO	NOTES

Routines and Predictability

Routines and having a predictable life can help manage anxious thoughts and unnecessary stress. How do you find Mornings or evening with regards to your tics?

Create an ideal schedule for the day ahead each morning

TIME	TO DO	NOTES

Routines and Predictability

Routines and having a predictable life can help manage anxious thoughts and unnecessary stress. How do you find Mornings or evening with regards to your tics?

You may prefer to break your day into three parts

Routines and Predictability

Routines and having a predictable life can help manage anxious thoughts and unnecessary stress. How do you find Mornings or evening with regards to your tics?

You may prefer to break your day into three parts

Routines and Predictability

Routines and having a predictable life can help manage anxious thoughts and unnecessary stress. How do you find Mornings or evening with regards to your tics?

You may prefer to break your day into three parts

Additional Notes and Doodles

Additional Notes and Doodles

Additional Notes and Doodles

Additional Notes and Doodles

Additional Notes and Doodles

Additional Notes and Doodles

Additional Notes and Doodles

Additional Notes and Doodles

Additional Notes and Doodles

Additional Notes and Doodles

Additional Notes and Doodles

Additional Notes and Doodles

Additional Notes and Doodles

Additional Notes and Doodles

Additional Notes and Doodles

EDUCATE
EMPOWER
ADVOCATE

Additional Notes and Doodles

Quiz Answers

```
S E A S T B R R C T I C
N E U R O L O G I C A L
I N V O L U N T A R Y G
F P O C O I O C S C A R
M O T O R L R E O H B D
O H S H O G T T R B B O
V E S E E T V A P O I P
E R D T E T I R I N G A
M V N R S G E T C I R M
E P U E O S N S E C R I
N O O V O C A L G R R N
T H S S T H T E U R G E
```

```
        ¹T I R ²E D
              X
       ³C H R O N I C
        R         I
  ⁴T O ⁶U R E T T ⁵E S    ⁷T R A N S I E N T
   I    R         Y        I
   C    G         E        R
        E         R        E
                  O        D
        A         L
        T
        I
        V
        E
```

Made in the USA
Coppell, TX
25 April 2023

16045610R00057